AMAZING
OPTICAL
ILLUSIONS

IllusionWorks

FIREFLY BOOKS

A FIREFLY BOOK

Published by Firefly Books Ltd., 2004
All images and text © 2004 IllusionWorks, L.L.C. except:
Ames Room (page 7) © Exploratorium;
Legs of two different genders (page 24) © Shigeo Fukuda;
Impossible terrace (page 15) © David MacDonald.

First Printing

Publisher Cataloging-in-Publication Data (U.S.)
Amazing optical illusions / IllusionWorks.
[32] p. : col. ill. ; cm.
Summary: Collection of 32 optical illusions rendered in photography, artwork and computer imaging.
ISBN 1-55297-961-X
ISBN 1-55297-962-8 (pbk.)
1. Optical illusions — Juvenile literature. I. IllusionWorks.
II. Title.
152.14/8 22   QP495.A439 2004

Published in the United States in 2004 by
Firefly Books (U.S.) Inc.
P.O. Box 1338, Ellicott Station
Buffalo, New York 14205

National Library of Canada Cataloguing in Publication
Amazing optical illusions / IllusionWorks.

ISBN 1-55297-961-X (bound).—ISBN 1-55297-962-8 (pbk.)
1. Optical illusions—Juvenile literature. I. IllusionWorks
QP495.A42 2004   j152.14'8   C2004-902569-4

To Paul MacCready

Published in Canada in 2004 by
Firefly Books Ltd.
66 Leek Crescent
Richmond Hill, Ontario L4B 1H1

Printed in Canada

The Publisher acknowledges the financial support of the Government of Canada through the Book Publishing Industry Development Program for its publishing activities.

EYE TRICKED YOU!

MOST of us don't think too much about our amazing sense of sight. It seems to work automatically, but it doesn't. How do we sort out what we see? Most of that job is done by our brain and not our eyes!

When you see something, light enters your eyes. The light is focused on sensitive "screens" at the back of each eyeball. The information focused there is sent to your brain. Then it's your brain's job to make sense out of the information it gets.

This is where optical illusions come in. "Optical" has to do with your sight. An "illusion" is a kind of trick. When you look at an optical illusion, some part of the process just doesn't match up. This may happen because of how the eye works. It may also happen because of how the brain works. So you may see things that really aren't there or that just don't make sense!

Much of the fun of this book involves "playing" with your sense of sight so you are fooled. It has nothing to do with how smart you are or how old you are. You will be tricked.

To get the most out of this book, read the question at the top of the page. Then look at the picture. Do your best to "figure it out" before looking at the descriptions at the bottom of the page.

Now, go have some fun!

What is this a picture of?

There are actually two pictures here. If you look at the white area, you will see a vase. If you look at the green areas, you will see two faces in profile. At any one time you can only see either the faces or the vase.

Can you see the arrows?

Depending on how you look at it, this is a picture of arrows or of men running.

What is hiding here?

It's a Dalmatian dog. Once you have seen the hidden image, you will be able to separate the spotted dog from the spotted background. You will never be able to see this picture in its meaningless form again.

Are the two kids in this room the same height?

Yes they are. The illusion occurs because unlike most rooms, this one is not shaped like a cube. In this room, the left corner (where the girl is) is twice as far away as the right corner (where the boy is). It is also at a lower height. From this angle, however, the two corners appear to be about the same distance away and the floor appears level.

Does this picture make sense?

Cover up the right half and then cover up the left half. You will find that each end makes sense. But when you uncover the two "possible" halves you will end up with an impossible figure.

What do you see here?

This image of a basset hound was made from a collage of animal images. If you look at the picture from far away, you will see the dog. From close up, you will see all the little pictures that make up the dog image.

Can you make these hands touch?

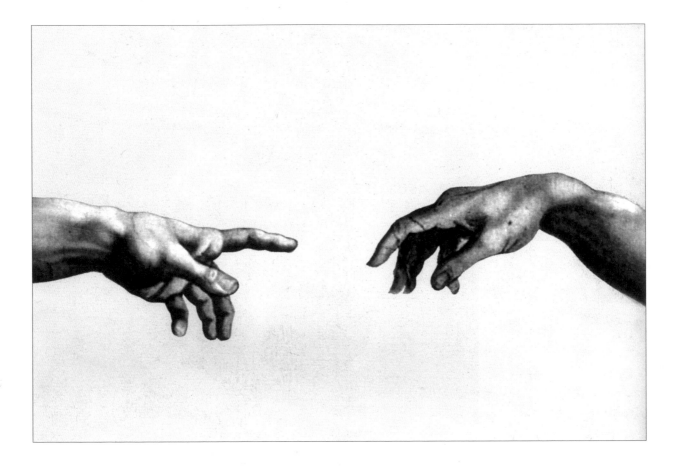

It's a miracle! Look at this illustration with both eyes and bring the page slowly toward your face. The hands will touch!

What happened to these houses?

No, these houses have not collapsed. They are located on a very steep street in San Francisco. The photographer created the illusion by tilting the camera so that it was level with the street. The woman adds to the illusion. She isn't standing straight. Instead, she is leaning in the same direction as the tilted camera.

Who broke the bookshelves?

No one. Look closely. These shelves only appear to be falling.

Do you see a spiral?

What you see appears to be a spiral, but it is really a series of perfect circles! The black-and-white "twist" of each circle is what produces the spiral effect.

Which face appears happier?

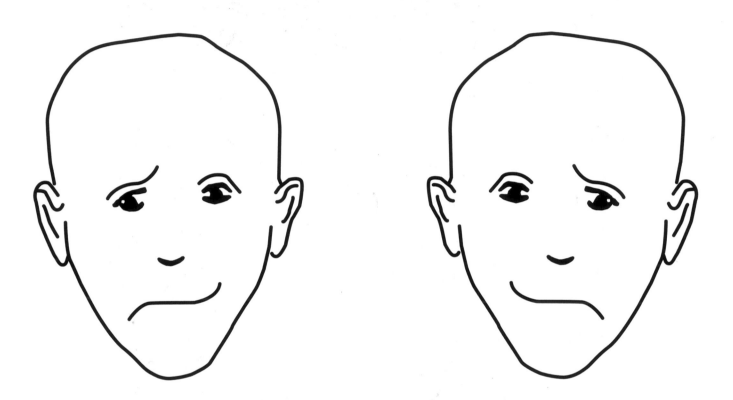

Many people see the right face as happier. However, neither face is really "happier" than the other. They are mirror-images.

Are you looking at this structure from above or below?

Both — and neither! If you cover up either the top or bottom half, you will find that each end is perfectly possible. But when you uncover the two "possible" halves you end up with an impossible image. Notice how the ladder twists in an impossible way.

Is there anything wrong with this picture?

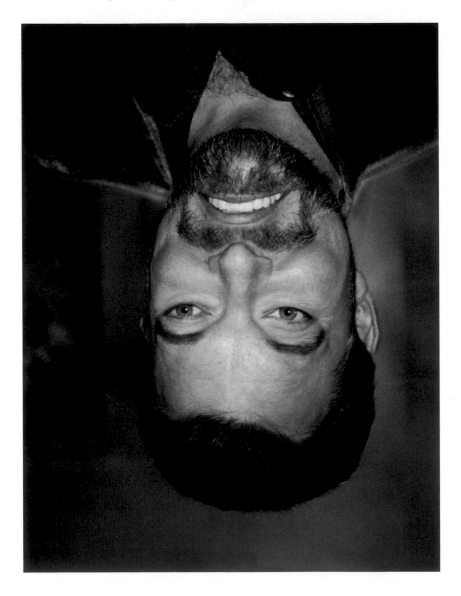

This image of actor Jonathan Frakes does not look too scary until you turn the picture upside down. Then you can see that the eyes and mouth have been turned around.

What will this young man look like when he gets older?

Turn the image upside down to find out.

Do you see spots before your eyes?

This illusion looks a little different if you change color of the squares. For example, if the squares were black then you would see ghostly gray dots. If you look directly at any dot, it will disappear.

Which is the shadow and which is the cat?

The image on the left is the shadow, and the one on the
right is the cat. Turn this page on its side to be sure.

How many children can you count?

The artist has drawn this picture so there are only five heads, If you try hard, you can count ten children.

Is the small man standing in the bottom-right corner the same size as the man at the very back?

Yes, he is the same size. This is called a perspective illusion. It shows how two of the same objects can look different depending on their position.

Do you know how to make a finger float right before your eyes?

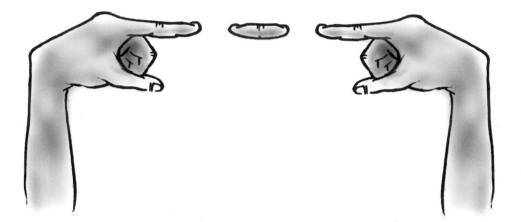

Hold your two hands in front of your face. Keep the tips of your index fingers slightly apart and at eye level. Focus on a wall several feet behind your fingers. You should see a floating piece of finger. If you focus on your fingers instead of the wall, the illusion vanishes.

Can you see the circles moving at different speeds?

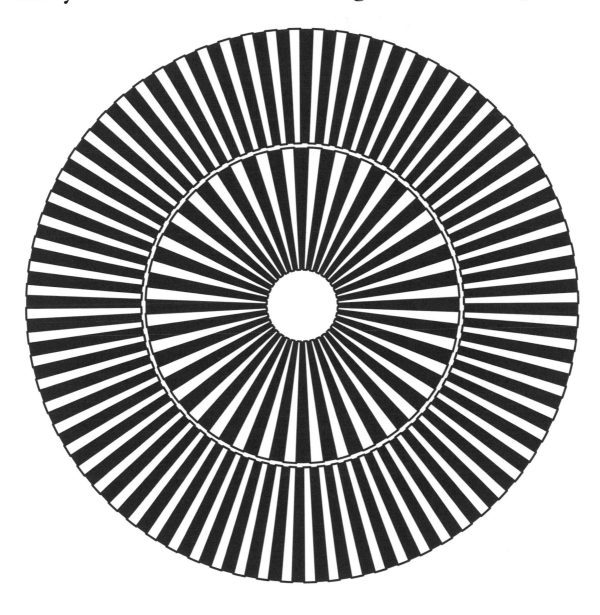

Look at this picture while moving the page in wide circles. Don't change the direction of the figure. You should see the two circles move at different rates of speed.

Are these men's legs or women's legs?

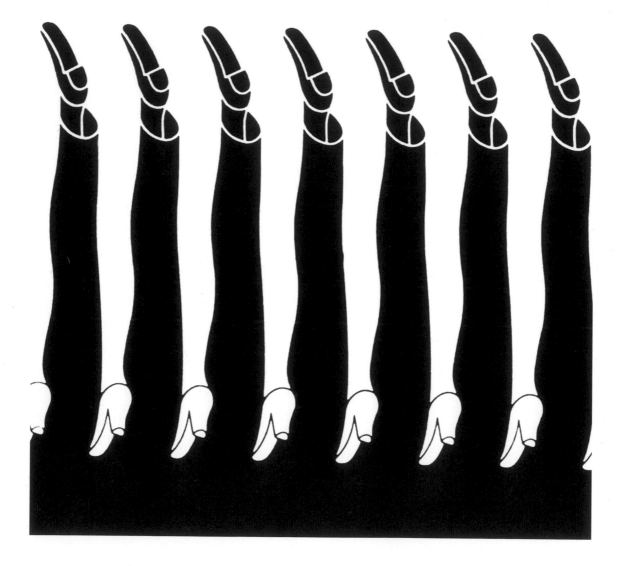

Both! Look at just the blue areas and then just the white areas. Can you see the different legs?

How many tools can you find?

Look at both the white areas and colored areas. There are over a dozen tools here, including a handsaw, a pair of pliers and a shovel.

The balls are in exactly the same position. The shadows in the second illustration make them appear higher in that picture.

Do you see flashing dots?

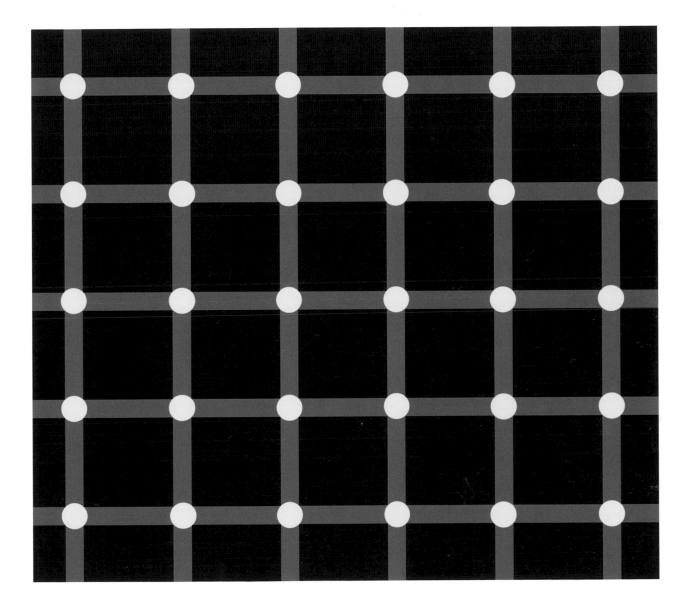

The circles appear to flash when you move your eyes around this image.
Nobody completely understands what causes this effect.

Has the elephant lost its legs?

This elephant will have trouble walking because of the way the artist has drawn him.

Which line appears longer, the red or blue line?

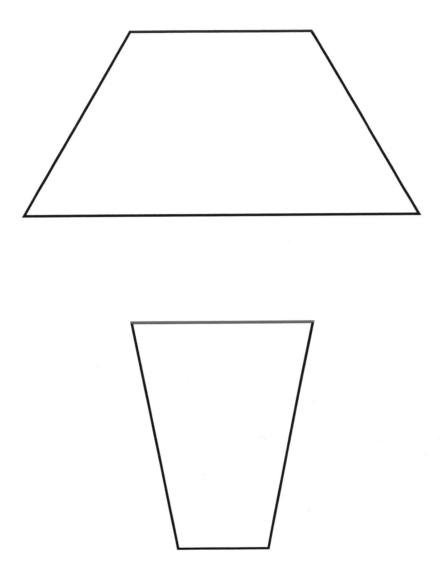

The red line appears slightly longer than the blue line, even though they are both exactly the same length. Measure them both and you'll see.

Is this a picture of fruit or a portrait?

Look closely. Depending on how you look at it, you can see either a bunch of fruit or a portrait of Emperor Rudolf II. The Emperor loved this portrait, which was painted in the late 1500s by Italian artist Giuseppe Arcimboldo.

Is this really a spiral?

Although it looks like a spiral, it isn't. A series of circles creates this illusion.

Are the black lines straight or curved?

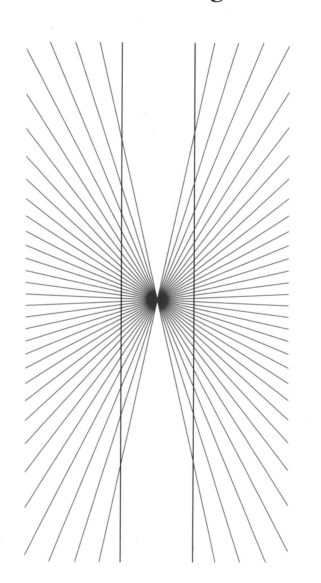

They are perfectly straight. The pattern of blue lines creates the illusion that the black lines curve outward.